CAN YOU IMAGINE?

Being a

SLOTH

By Julia McDonnell

Gareth Stevens
Publishing

Please visit our website, www.garethstevens.com. For a free color catalog of all our high-quality books, call toll free 1-800-542-2595 or fax 1-877-542-2596.

Library of Congress Cataloging-in-Publication Data

McDonnell, Julia.
Being a sloth / by Julia McDonnell.
 p. cm. — (Can you imagine?)
Includes index.
ISBN 978-1-4824-3274-9 (pbk.)
ISBN 978-1-4824-3275-6 (6-pack)
ISBN 978-1-4824-0099-1 (library binding)
1. Sloths — Juvenile literature. I. McDonnell, Julia, 1979- II. Title.
QL737.E2 M38 2014
599.313—dc23

First Edition

Published in 2014 by
Gareth Stevens Publishing
111 East 14th Street, Suite 349
New York, NY 10003

Designer: Katelyn E. Reynolds
Editor: Therese Shea

Photo credits: Cover, p. 1 Willie Davis/Shutterstock.com; cover, pp. 1–32 (background texture) AnnabelleaDesigns/Shutterstock.com; pp. 5, 7 (inset), 13, 17, 19, 21 iStockphoto/Thinkstock.com; p. 7 (main) Vilainecrevette/Shutterstock.com; p. 9 Feargus Cooney/Lonely Planet Images/Getty Images; p. 10 Hoberman Collection/Universal Images Group/Getty Images; p. 11 (inset) Eric Isselee/Shutterstock.com; p. 11 (main) Photo Researchers/Getty Images; p. 15 Tom Brakefield/Stockbyte/Thinkstock.com; p. 23 Visuals Unlimited, Inc./Andres Morya/Getty Images; p. 24 Kjersti Joergensen/Shutterstock.com; p. 25 BMJ/Shutterstock.com; p. 27 (inset) Andy Poole/Shutterstock.com; p. 27 (main) MaViLa/Flickr/Getty Images; p. 29 Waltraud Grubitzsch/AFP/Getty Images.

Printed in the United States of America

CPSIA compliance information: Batch #CW14GS: For further information contact Gareth Stevens, New York, New York at 1-800-542-2595.

CONTENTS

Words in the glossary appear in **bold** type the first time they are used in the text.

CAN YOU HANG?

Imagine living in a rainforest, spending most of your life up in the trees. You hang upside down—even when eating and sleeping. You can thank the long claws on your four feet for that. Your back legs are so weak that you can't walk.

You're very slow moving, and people use your name as another word for a lazy person. Your fur can become covered with **algae**. It may even have other creatures living in it. You've just pictured yourself as a sloth!

imagine that!

Two-toed sloths are also called unau (yoo-NAW). Three-toed sloths are called ai (AH-ee).

Sloths are so well **camouflaged** that predators sometimes think they're just part of a tree.

5

FUNNY-LOOKING ANIMALS

If you were a sloth, most people would think you're unusual looking. Sloths have long front legs and shorter back legs. Each toe has a hook-like claw. Their shaggy coats are shades of brown or gray. Their fur looks a bit like long hair.

Sloths' round heads and flat faces hold small eyes and tiny ears, neither of which are very helpful. Sloths rely more on their short **snout**. They have an excellent sense of smell.

imagine that!

If a sloth has an orange or yellow patch of fur between its shoulders, it's a male.

Some sloths have a mouth that turns up. They look like they're always smiling!

male sloth

7

GIANT SLOTHS!

If you were a sloth, your family tree would stretch back about 60 million years! The **ancestors** of today's sloths were cat-sized, tree-dwelling **mammals** in what is now South America. Since there were few predators that ate them, some began to live on the ground.

The ground sloths grew in size—some as big as elephants! They walked on all fours and stood on their back legs to reach plants. However, giant ground sloths died out. Their smaller relatives who remained in the trees became the sloths we know.

imagine that!

The remains of ground sloths, including hair and skin, have been found in caves!

The skeleton of a South American giant sloth shows how different they were from the sloths we see today. A giant ground sloth's claws were 7 inches (18 cm) long!

9

TWO TOES OR THREE?

Most sloths are very similar. However, they're separated into two groups based on whether they have two or three toes on their front "feet." In general, the two-toed sloths are larger, faster, and nocturnal, which means they're active at night. The three-toed sloths are smaller, slower, and active both during the day and night.

If you were a sloth and you couldn't count, look for your tail. If you can spot a small one, you're a three-toed sloth. If you don't have a tail, you're a two-toed sloth.

imagine that!

A three-toed sloth can turn its head almost all the way around!

Can you tell which is the two-toed sloth and which is the three-toed sloth?

11

TREE DWELLERS

If you were a sloth, you'd live in the warm, wet rainforests of Central and South America. A rainforest has different layers. The tops of the trees are called the emergent layer. The next two layers are the canopy and the understory. Sloths live in these layers because they provide plenty of food, water, and camouflage.

Sloths move to the lowest layer, the forest floor, about once a week. However, they climb back up as soon as possible.

imagine that!

Sloths can't wiggle their toes separately like people can. That's because their toes are all connected.

Sloths are arboreal (ahr-BOHR-ee-uhl). That means they live in trees.

13

LIFE UPSIDE DOWN

Sloths spend most of their time upside down. Their long, curved claws are amazing tools that let them do just about everything "wrong side up." While eating upside down may seem unusual but not impossible for us, sloths also **mate** and give birth that way.

Some sloths tuck themselves among branches to rest, but most even sleep hanging from trees. Sloths have been found hanging upside down in branches after they've died! If you like to hang from monkey bars, can you imagine doing that all day?

imagine that!

A sloth's fur grows from its stomach to its back so that rain can run off.

A Hoffman's two-toed sloth hangs by its back feet.

15

ON THE MENU

Sloths are mainly herbivores (UHR-buh-vohrz). That means they eat plants. Both two-toed and three-toed sloths eat leaves and twigs, but two-toed sloths also enjoy fruits, bugs, and sometimes eggs. Two-toed sloths move to a different tree to eat each night. Three-toed sloths eat late in the day and stay in a smaller area.

All sloths grind down their food with their hard teeth. The **bacteria** in their stomach break the food down more. If you were a sloth, this process might take a month!

imagine that!

Because they get worn down by chewing, a sloth's teeth never stop growing.

A three-toed sloth eats a meal in Costa Rica.

17

SLOW BUT STEADY

Sloths don't have much **muscle** compared to other mammals, so they don't need to eat or drink as much to keep their body working. They don't have to spend a lot of their time searching for food, so they rest much of the day.

As a sloth, your plant diet wouldn't provide many **nutrients**, so your slow speed would help save energy. When sloths need to travel, they use a hand-over-hand motion in trees. On the ground, they drag themselves using their front legs.

imagine that!

Sloths are three times faster in the water than on land and can hold their breath underwater for 40 minutes!

A three-toed sloth uses its claws to pull itself across the ground.

Sloths, Side by Side

two-toed sloths

length: 24 to 27 inches (61 to 69 cm)

weight: up to 18 pounds (8 kg)

active: nocturnal

tail: none visible

diet: leaves, twigs, fruits, bugs, eggs

three-toed sloths

length: up to 23 inches (58 cm)

weight: less than 9 pounds (4 kg)

active: both day and night

tail: small tail

diet: leaves, twigs

19

COOL CREATURES

Most mammals' body temperature stays much the same, no matter their surroundings. Sloths' body temperature can change a lot. If you were a sloth, your temperature might change from 74°F to 92°F (23°C to 33°C)! This change would be very dangerous in a person's body.

When sloths are cold, they slow down even more than usual and use the sun's rays to warm themselves, similar to what **reptiles** do. When they become too warm, they move to a shaded spot to cool down.

imagine that!

One study found that sloths sleep 6 hours less per day in the wild than in **captivity**. Wild sloths stay awake to watch for predators and seek food.

A three-toed sloth warms itself in a patch of sun.

21

SLOTH FAMILIES

If you were a sloth, you'd live on your own. Though some two-toed sloth females live in small groups, most sloths meet only when it's mating time.

Mother and baby sloths are never lonely. They spend just about all their time together. Just after birth, a newborn sloth holds tightly to its mother's hair. She teaches it which plants to eat, and it learns how to hang upside down. Young sloths stay with their mother from 6 months to 2 years.

imagine that!

A female sloth usually has one baby per year.

A Hoffman's two-toed sloth mother cradles her baby.

23

A HOME FOR OTHERS

Can you imagine having plantlike things and tiny animals living in your hair? Since sloths are such slow movers, their fur is an ideal place for tiny creatures to live. Green algae may look yucky, but algae help sloths blend in with their forest surroundings. Algae can also be a snack!

Algae aren't just a meal for the sloths. One sloth may have hundreds of bugs, such as beetles and moths, living on it. Some eat the algae, and others, like ticks, feed on the sloths themselves.

This three-toed sloth blends in with the forest canopy.

25

FACING DANGERS

Sloths' thick skin, heavy coat, and sharp claws offer some protection. However, the easiest way for them to avoid danger is to stay still in trees. But if you were a sloth, you'd still have to watch out for predators.

Harpy eagles try to pull sloths from their hiding spots. Big cats called jaguars can climb trees in search of prey. On the ground, sloths are easy targets for **ocelots**. In the water, **anacondas** can surprise a sloth. Some humans even hunt sloths for their meat and fur.

imagine that!

In the wild, sloths usually live about 10 to 15 years. Those in captivity often live longer.

This sloth's fur is a good match to this tree's bark.

ocelot

27

LOOKING TO THE FUTURE

The destruction of rainforests means sloths face more dangers. These include loss of food, less chance to meet other sloths to mate, and fewer trees to provide safe homes. Because of their limited diet, sloths have a hard time living in new places, even zoos.

However, sloths have been around for millions of years, and many of their populations are still strong. So, if you like trees and a slow-moving life, go ahead and imagine yourself as a sloth! Hopefully these animals will be around for many years to come.

This sloth in a German zoo is 40 years old!

29

GLOSSARY

algae: living plantlike things that are mostly found in water

anaconda: a large South American snake that lives in or near water and in trees

ancestor: an animal that lived before others in its family tree

bacteria: tiny creatures that can only be seen with a microscope

camouflage: to use colors or shapes to blend in with surroundings

captivity: the state of being caged

mammal: a warm-blooded animal that has a backbone and hair, breathes air, and feeds milk to its young

mate: one of two animals that come together to make babies. Also, to come together to make babies.

muscle: one of the parts of the body that allow movement

nutrient: something a living thing needs to grow and stay alive

ocelot: a small wildcat with dark spots on a light brown coat

reptile: an animal covered with scales or plates that breathes air, has a backbone, and lays eggs, such as a turtle, snake, lizard, or crocodile

snout: an animal's nose and mouth

FOR MORE INFORMATION

Books

Miller, Sara Swan. *Sloths*. New York, NY: PowerKids Press, 2008.

Piehl, Janet. *Let's Look at Sloths*. Minneapolis, MN: Lerner, 2011.

Stewart, Melissa. *Sloths*. Minneapolis, MN: Carolrhoda Books, 2005.

Websites

Animal Diversity Web
animaldiversity.ummz.umich.edu/
Search this website and learn about many different kinds of sloths.

Sloths
kids.nationalgeographic.com/kids/animals/creaturefeature/sloths/
Read why a sloth would always be late for school and more fun facts!

INDEX